Transylvania

Travel Guide

2024

Unveiling Legends, Castles, and Hidden Gems in Romania's Mysterious Region

Jayden Gray

TO GAIN ACCESS TO MORE BOOKS FROM JAYDEN GRAY, PLEASE SCAN THIS QR CODE

Table of Contents

About This Guide

Welcome to the "Transylvania Travel Guide 2024," your guide for exploring the enchanting region of Transylvania. This book is intended to make your trip to Transylvania as memorable and pleasurable as possible by assisting you in discovering the region's rich history, stunning scenery, and dynamic culture.

What You'll Find Inside

Everything you need to know to plan your Transylvanian journey is written in this book, including:

- Details about Transylvania's geography, history, and culture will help you better appreciate the area's rich legacy.
- Helpful advice on when to go, where to stay, and how to get about can make your vacation easy and peaceful.

- Transylvania's top attractions, things to do, and undiscovered treasures will help you make the most of your stay.
- Practical information and useful phrases in Romanian will help you interact with people and fully experience the culture.

The "Transylvania Travel Guide 2024" is your pass to an amazing journey across one of the most intriguing parts of Europe. This book provides all the information you need to make your vacation to Transylvania unforgettable, regardless of whether you're an experienced tourist or a first-time visitor. Prepare to discover the enchantment of Transylvania in 2024 by packing your luggage and grabbing a copy of the handbook.

Introduction to Transylvania

Transylvania, a name wrapped in mystery and interest, conjures images of gothic castles, misty mountains, and ancient folklore. This ancient area, which is in the center of Romania, is a beautiful place with a rich cultural legacy.

History of Transylvania

The history of Transylvania is just as complex and captivating as the country itself. It has been influenced by many different civilizations throughout the ages, including the Romans, Hungarians, Saxons, and Ottomans, as well as the ancient Dacians. Transylvania joined Romania in the 19th century; the two countries formally united during World War I.

The story of Dracula, which has endured for centuries in Transylvania, is based on the life of Vlad the Impaler, a medieval ruler renowned for using cruel methods to subdue his adversaries. The area became even more iconic in popular culture because of Bram Stoker's "Dracula," which attracted tourists from all over the globe who were drawn to its mysterious and sinister history.

Geography of Transylvania

Transylvania, an area of remarkable natural beauty, lies tucked away in the center of Romania. The dominant feature of the area is the Carpathian Mountains, which provide amazing views and fantastic hiking possibilities. In addition, the area has charming towns, glistening rivers, and thick woods, all of which combine to create a scenery that seems taken from a fairy tale.

The cities of Transylvania, with their ancient architecture, cobblestone streets, and lively cultural scenes, are just as charming. Transylvania has a rich history and beautiful cities, among which include Cluj-Napoca, Brasov, and Sibiu.

Culture of Transylvania

Transylvania's culture is a synthesis of several historical influences. Saxon, Roma, Hungarian, and Romanian cultures have all influenced the distinctive personality of the area. Transylvania is a wonderful area to visit because of its diverse architecture, food, and customs, all of which reflect this variety.

People from Transylvania are renowned for their warmth and friendliness, and they provide a warm welcome to guests. Customary celebrations, including the Sibiu International Theatre Festival and the Transylvanian Film Festival, highlight the area's thriving cultural sector and provide a window into its rich creative past.

Reasons to Go Visit Transylvania in 2024

The charm of Transylvania is its capacity to take travelers to a place that seems both timeless and old. In 2024, the area will enthrall tourists with its distinct fusion of natural beauty, history, and culture.

Touring the many castles and strongholds in Transylvania is one of the attractions of the region. Both Peles Castle, a magnificent example of neo-renaissance architecture, and Bran Castle, which is often linked to the Dracula legend, are must-sees. In addition, the area is home to several historic towns, such as Sibiu and Brașov, where tourists may meander along cobblestone streets and experience a bygone era.

Transylvania has many attractions for those who adore the outdoors. Numerous national parks, including the Retezat National Park and the Piatra Craiului National Park, are located in the area. Here, tourists may trek, ride, and take in the breathtaking natural scenery.

Transylvania is a place that has something to offer everyone regardless of your interests—history, culture, or just taking in the breathtaking natural beauty. Transylvania is sure to enchant and delight. So why wait? Start planning your trip to Transylvania in 2024 and discover the magic of this captivating region for yourself.

Planning Your Trip to Transylvania

To guarantee a seamless and remarkable trip, careful preparation is necessary before departing for Transylvania.

Best Time to Visit Transylvania

Your interests and the activities you want to engage in will determine when is the ideal time to visit Transylvania. There are four different seasons in the area, and each has its special appeal.

- **Spring (March–May):** With the countryside bursting with vivid hues, spring is a great time to explore Transylvania. Because of the moderate weather, it's perfect for outdoor pursuits like hiking and town exploration.

- **Summer (June-August):** With its mild weather and longer days, summer is Transylvania's busiest travel season. Now is the ideal time to see the outdoor attractions and castles in the area. But be ready for greater pricing and crowds.

- **Autumn (September–November):** As the leaves change color, autumn provides Transylvania with a blast of color. It's a perfect time to go hiking and take in the natural beauty of the area since the temperature is still good.

- **Winter (December–February):** With snow-covered landscapes and charming Christmas markets, winter turns Transylvania into a wintry paradise. Experience the winter sports and festive customs of the area at this lovely time of year.

Visa Requirements and Entry Regulations

Finding out about the criteria for a visa and entrance restrictions is often the first step in planning a trip to Transylvania for many tourists. Though it is not yet a part of the Schengen Area, Romania is a member of the European Union. As a result, Romania may have different visa requirements than other EU nations.

Foreign visitors should confirm well in advance of their journey to Romania what kind of visa they need. Generally speaking, a visa is needed for visits longer than ninety days or for specific objectives like employment or education.

Travel Essentials

You may increase the comfort and enjoyment of your vacation to Transylvania by packing appropriately. The following are some things you may want to pack:

- **Clothing:** Bring clothes appropriate for the activity and season you want to engage in. It's important to wear layers, particularly in the winter. Remember to bring comfortable footwear while visiting the area's castles and scenic spots.

- **Travel Documents:** Make sure you have all the paperwork you'll need for your trip, such as your passport, visa (if applicable), travel insurance, and any pertinent health records.

- **Electronics:** Don't forget to bring your smartphone or camera so you can document Transylvania's breathtaking scenery and ancient places. Keeping your gadgets charged while on the road may also be accomplished using a portable charger.

- **Medications:** Bring a basic first-aid kit and any prescription drugs you may need. Having a copy of your medications with you is also a good idea in case you need to fill them while on the road.

- **Other Necessities:** You should also think about bringing sunscreen, bug repellant, a travel adaptor and reusable water bottles to keep hydrated while sightseeing,

While organizing a trip to Transylvania, it's important to think about the ideal time to go, the necessary travel documents, and the conditions for obtaining a visa. You can make sure that your trip to this fascinating area goes smoothly and pleasantly by taking the time to prepare beforehand.

Getting to Transylvania

Located in the center of Romania, Transylvania is a mesmerizing travel destination with breathtaking scenery and a fascinating past. Several transit alternatives make it easy to reach this wonderful place.

Flights to Transylvania

The most convenient way to reach Transylvania from international destinations is by flying into one of the region's airports. Transylvania's primary airports are:

1. Cluj-Napoca International Airport (CLJ)
Address: Strada Traian Vuia 149-151, Cluj-Napoca 400397, Romania
The main airport in Transylvania is close to Cluj-Napoca and serves both local and international flights. Airlines that regularly fly

to Cluj-Napoca include Tarom, Wizz Air, and Lufthansa.

2. Sibiu International Airport (SBZ)

Address: Șoseaua Alba Iulia 73, Sibiu 550052, Romania

Located close to Sibiu, this airport acts as a point of entry for visitors coming from all across Europe into Transylvania. Sibiu is served by flights operated by airlines including Blue Air, Wizz Air, and Lufthansa.

3. Târgu Mureș Transylvania Airport

Address: Ungheni 547605, Romania

This airport, which is close to Târgu Mureș, serves both local and international travel, mostly to locations in Europe. Airlines that fly to Târgu Mureș include Tarom and Wizz Air.

Trains to Transylvania

The picturesque and comfortable train ride to Transylvania is a great chance to take in the splendor of the country. Transylvania's principal cities and towns are connected to other regions of Romania and Europe by trains that run on a well-developed network. Among the principal rail stations in Transylvania are:

1. Cluj-Napoca Railway Station
Address: Strada Căii Ferate, Cluj-Napoca 400394, Romania
Situated in the city's heart, this station serves as a significant Transylvanian rail hub. This is where trains from Timișoara, Bucharest, and other Romanian cities arrive and leave.

2. Sibiu Railway Station
Address: Piața 1 Decembrie 1918, Sibiu 550200, Romania

This station, which is close to the city center, is a major transit hub for tourists visiting Sibiu and neighboring regions of Transylvania.

3. Braşov Train Station
Address: Bulevardul Gării 1A, Braşov 500148, Romania

This station, which is in the heart of the city, is well-liked by visitors who are taking in Brasov and its surrounding' historic beauty.

Buses to Transylvania

Bus travel to Transylvania is also a practical choice, particularly for those on a tight budget. Numerous bus companies provide frequent trips to and from Transylvania, linking the region's main cities and communities. Among the principal bus stops in Transylvania are:

1. Cluj-Napoca Autogara
Address: Cluj-Napoca 400124, Romania

This bus station, which is close to the city center, serves several locations in Romania and other countries, making it an important hub for bus travel in Transylvania.

2. Autogara Sibiu Vest Curse Internationale
Address: Strada Europa Unită 11, Sibiu 550018, Romania

This bus station is located close to the city center and provides services to locations in Transylvania and other regions of Romania.

3. Autogara Internationala Stadionul Municipal Brașov
Address: Calea Făgărașului 39, Brașov, Romania

This bus terminal, which is in the heart of the city, is a handy place to start your bus tour of Brasov and its environments.

Travel Tips for Getting About Transylvania

1. Public Transportation: Buses and trams are among the many modes of public transportation that are readily available in Transylvania's cities and villages. Tickets may be bought on board or via kiosks; it's a good idea to prepare some spare coins.

2. Car Rental: Taking a rental car is a fantastic option to get about Transylvania at your speed. Before you go behind the wheel, however, make sure you are conversant with the traffic laws and ordinances in your area.

3. Cycling: Cycling lovers will find Transylvania to be an excellent visit due to its stunning scenery. You may discover the beauty of the area on two wheels by renting a bike from one of the many cities and villages in the area.

4. Taxis: While you can easily find taxis in Transylvania's cities and towns, it's a good idea to choose reliable taxi services and settle on a price before you go.

5. Language: Although English and other languages are often spoken, particularly in tourist regions, Romanian is the official language of the country.

Car, Bicycle and Motorcycle Rentals in Transylvania

It's a pleasure to explore Transylvania's scenic landscapes, attractive towns, and ancient monuments at your speed. You may explore the area's gorgeous pathways and hidden wonders at your own pace by renting a bicycle or automobile.

Car Rental in Transylvania

When visiting Transylvania, tourists who want to see the many attractions in the area sometimes choose to rent a vehicle. Transylvania is home to several domestic and foreign automobile rental companies that provide a large selection of cars to fit a variety of demands and price ranges. Several of Transylvania's leading automobile rental companies are:

1. Avis Aeroport Cluj

Address: Strada Traian Vuia 149-151, Cluj-Napoca 400397, Romania

In Transylvania, Avis has many rental sites, including major centers and airports. They provide a range of automobiles, from premium to affordable models.

2. Thrifty

Address: Sibiu International Airport Arrivals Hall, Sibiu 550052, Romania

Thrifty offers a variety of cars for hire at its rental sites throughout Transylvania's main cities and villages. Long-term and one-way rental options are also provided.

3. Europcar Rent a Car Brasov
Address: Strada 13 Decembrie 31, Brașov 500199, Romania

Transylvania is home to Europcar rental stations offering a variety of cars for hire. They provide alternatives for extra services like kid seats and GPS guidance.

Bicycle and Motorcycle Rental in Transylvania

A popular method to see the stunning scenery and towns of Transylvania is by bicycle o. In Transylvania, you may hire mountain bikes, road bikes, and electric bikes from several rental companies. Among the major companies in Transylvania that hire bicycles are:

1. Transylvania Cycling
Address: Dretea 407374, Cluj-Napoca, Romania

Transylvania Cycling, based in Cluj-Napoca, provides guided cycling trips across the area in addition to a variety of bicycles for hire.

2. Transylvania Moto Experience
Address: Strada Ecaterina Varga 24, Brașov, Romania

Transylvania Moto Experience, a Brașov-based company, offers motorbike rentals for touring the city and its environs.

3. Bike Rentals Sibiu - Light Cycling Transylvania
Address: Strada VIII 4, Cristian 557085, Romania

City bikes and mountain bikes are among the bicycles available for hire at Sibiu Bike Rental.

Travel Tips for Renting a Car, Motorcycle, or Bicycle in Transylvania

1. Plan Ahead: To guarantee availability, make reservations for your rental bicycle or vehicle well in advance during the busiest travel seasons.

2. Examine Insurance Coverage: Before renting a car, confirm the insurance coverage offered by the rental company and, if necessary, look at acquiring supplemental insurance.

3. Learn the Traffic Laws: Before driving or riding a bicycle, it's vital to get acquainted with the traffic laws in Transylvania, since they may vary from those in your native country.

4. Examine the Vehicle: Check the rental vehicle or bicycle for any damage and make sure all of the required accessories, including locks and lights, are operational before accepting it.

5. Stay Safe: Put safety first at all times, whether you're riding or driving. When riding, wear a helmet; when driving, abide by the traffic laws; and always be alert of your surroundings.

Transylvania is easily and conveniently accessible, offering a variety of transportation choices. You'll have an amazing trip to this fascinating area whether you decide to fly, ride the train, or take a bus.

Additionally, renting a car, a motorcycle, or a bicycle in Transylvania offers a practical and adaptable means of taking in all the charm and beauty of the area. You're sure to discover the ideal choice for your trip to Transylvania with the variety of rental companies and automobiles available.

Exploring Transylvania's Cities and Towns

Numerous cities and towns in Transylvania, which is well-known for its breathtaking scenery and medieval beauty, provide a window into Romania's dynamic history and culture.

Cluj-Napoca: Cultural Capital of Transylvania

Cluj-Napoca, known for its dynamic cultural scene, old architecture, and young vitality, is regarded as Transylvania's cultural center. Cluj-Napoca was established in the second century AD by the Romans, and its many museums, galleries, and historic landmarks attest to its rich past.

Attractions in Cluj-Napoca

1. St. Michael's Church
Address: Piața Unirii, Cluj-Napoca 400015, Romania

With its tall spire and elaborate details, St. Michael's Church is one of Cluj-Napoca's most recognizable monuments and a magnificent example of Gothic architecture.

2. Central Park
Address: Parcul Central, Cluj-Napoca, Romania

With its rich vegetation, lake, and walking trails, Central Park is a well-liked meeting spot for both residents and tourists. It provides a peaceful getaway from the city.

3. Ethnographic Museum of Transylvania
Address: Memorandumului Str. 21, Cluj-Napoca 400114, Romania

This museum, which is housed in a stunning 16th-century structure, has displays of traditional crafts, costumes, and folklore to highlight Transylvania's cultural legacy.

4. Cluj-Napoca Botanical Garden

Address: Str. Republicii 42, Cluj-Napoca 400015, Romania

Established in 1872, this botanical garden has one of the biggest collections of plants from all over the globe, making it one of the biggest in Romania.

Getting to Cluj-Napoca

Cluj-Napoca is a significant center for transportation in Transylvania, with good bus and train service to neighboring cities. Depending on the route, traveling by rail or bus from Cluj-Napoca to places like Sibiu and Brașov takes three to four hours.

Brasov: Medieval Charm and Modern Delights

Brasov, a city tucked away in the Carpathian Mountains, is a perfect example of how to combine modern facilities with a rich medieval history. Brasov, which was established in the thirteenth century by the Teutonic Knights, has a rich past that is evident in its well-maintained historical buildings and landmarks.

Attractions in Brasov

1. The Council Square
Address: Brașov, Romania
Council Square, the center of Brasov's Old Town, is surrounded by stunning examples of medieval architecture and is home to the city's famous Council House, a representation of the city's medieval past.

2. The Black Church

Address: Curtea Johannes Honterus 2, Brașov 500025, Romania

The Black Church, one of Romania's biggest Gothic cathedrals, is a marvel of medieval architecture with an amazing collection of antiquities.

3. Mount Tampa

Address: Tâmpa, Brașov, Romania

Climb Mount Tampa or take the cable car to the summit for sweeping views of Brasov and the surrounding mountains. At the summit is a massive Hollywood-style sign.

Getting to Brasov

Major Romanian cities are readily reachable from Brasov by car, bus, or rail. It takes around three hours by rail or two and a half hours by driving to go from Bucharest to Brasov.

Sibiu: European Capital of Culture

Sibiu is sometimes referred to as the European Capital of Culture because of its strong cultural scene and well-preserved medieval buildings. Sibiu, which was founded in the twelfth century by German immigrants, has a rich past that is seen in its charming old town and important historical sites.

Attractions in Sibiu

1. Old Town
Address: Sibiu, Romania
The Old Town of Sibiu is a labyrinth of ancient structures, cobblestone alleyways, and attractive squares. Notable attractions include the Liar's Bridge and the Brukenthal National Museum.

2. ASTRA National Museum Complex

Address: Strada Pădurea Dumbrava 16, Sibiu 550399, Romania

Situated outside of Sibiu, this outdoor museum has displays of folk art, crafts, and architecture, portraying the way of life in a rural Romanian village.

3. Piatra Craiului National Park

Address: Ciocanu, Romania

This national park, which is just a short drive from Sibiu, has gorgeous hiking paths, quaint towns, and beautiful mountain views.

4. Sibiu Lutheran Cathedral

Address: Piata Albert Huet FN, Sibiu 550182, Romania

The Sibiu Lutheran Cathedral, a magnificent example of Gothic architecture, is a must-see for its breathtaking interior and expansive views from its tower.

Getting to Sibiu

Sibiu is well located for travel from Romania's main cities by automobile, bus, and rail. Approximately 4 hours may be spent traveling by rail or 3 hours driving from Cluj-Napoca to Sibiu.

Timișoara: Romania's Little Vienna

Timișoara, sometimes known as the Little Vienna of Romania, is a charming and elegant city. Timișoara is a charming ancient city that enthralls tourists with its stunning Baroque architecture, active cultural life, and relaxed vibe.

Attractions in Timișoara

1. Union Square
Address: Piața Unirii, Timișoara 300085, Romania

Union Square, the center of Timișoara's Old Town, is a hive of activity with lanes lined with vintage buildings, cafés, and restaurants.

2. Timișoara Orthodox Cathedral

Address: Bulevardul Regele Ferdinand I, Timișoara, Romania

The Timișoara Orthodox Cathedral, a magnificent specimen of Byzantine architecture, is a must-see for its exquisite interior and expansive views from its tower.

3. Victory Square

Address: Piața Victoriei, Timișoara, Romania

Victory Square, one of Timisoara's biggest squares, is the location of the Romanian Opera House and the Memorial Museum of the 1989 Revolution, among other significant monuments.

4. Timișoara Botanical Park

Address: Timișoara 300254, Romania

Timisoara Botanical Park is a serene haven in the middle of the city that is home to an extensive global plant collection.

Getting to Timișoara

Timișoara is well-served by major Romanian cities by rail, bus, and automobile. It takes around four hours by vehicle or five hours by rail to go from Bucharest to Timisoara.

Discovering the cities and villages of Transylvania provides an insight into Romania's dynamic culture and history. You will undoubtedly be enthralled with these amazing cities whether you begin your adventure in Cluj-Napoca, the cultural center of Romania, or are drawn to Timisoara's refinement, Sibiu's scene, or Brasov's historic beauty.

Legendary Castles and Fortresses

There are several renowned castles and strongholds in Transylvania that arouse curiosity and mystery. Starting with the well-known Bran Castle, the magnificent Peles Castle, Gothic Corvin Castle, and Râşnov Citadel Fortress. These architectural wonders are charming and rich in history.

1. Bran Castle: The Legendary Home of Dracula

Address: Strada General Traian Moşoiu 24, Bran 507025, Romania

One of Transylvania's most famous castles, Bran Castle is perched on a hill in the charming town of Bran. Bran Castle is rich in mythology and history, sometimes connected to the famous vampire Count Dracula.

History Bran Castle

Constructed in the fourteenth century, Bran Castle protected the mountain route that connected Wallachia and Transylvania as a strategic stronghold. The castle served as a royal home, a military fortress, and other functions throughout the ages.

Legend of Dracula

The reason Bran Castle is linked to the Dracula legend is because of its relationship to Vlad the Impaler, a medieval ruler infamous for using cruel methods to subdue his adversaries. Vlad never did reside at Bran Castle, but his association with the area has spawned many myths and tales, which have contributed to the castle's mythology as Dracula's residence.

Visiting Bran Castle

Nowadays, Bran Castle is a well-liked vacation spot that attracts travelers from all over the globe who are eager to explore its creepy tunnels and medieval chambers. A museum presenting the history and folklore of the area, with displays on Vlad the Impaler and the Dracula legend, is housed inside the castle.

2. Peles Castle: The Royal Jewel of Romania

Address: Aleea Peleșului 2, Sinaia 106100, Romania

One of the most beautiful castles in Europe, Peles Castle is a magnificent example of Neo-Renaissance architecture and is situated in the charming town of Sinaia. The Romanian royal family used Peles Castle, which was constructed in the late 19th century, as a vacation home.

History of Peles Castle

Peles Castle, commissioned by Romania's King Carol I, was created to highlight the nation's handicrafts and cultural legacy. This is shown by the inside of the castle, which has luxurious chambers with elaborate wood carvings, stained glass windows, and elaborate furniture.

Visiting Peles Castle

Peles Castle is accessible to the public today, enabling guests to enjoy its luxurious chambers and exquisite grounds. Every chamber in the castle provides a window into Romania's regal past, making its interior a veritable gold mine of artwork and history.

3. Corvin Castle: Hunedoara's Gothic Magnificence

Address: Strada Curtea Corvinilor 1-3, Hunedoara 331141, Romania

One of the most amazing medieval castles in Romania is Corvin Castle, sometimes called Hunyadi Castle or Hunedoara Castle. This magnificent castle, a monument to the rich history of the area and a masterpiece of Gothic construction, is situated in the Transylvanian town of Hunedoara.

History of Corvin Castle

One of the most powerful men in Hungary, John Hunyadi, constructed Corvin Castle in the fifteenth century. After being built as a fortification initially, the castle underwent renovations by succeeding owners to become a luxury home.

Design and Architecture

The Corvin castle, with its high walls, fortified towers, and graceful courtyards, is well known for its striking architecture and design. The inside of the castle is just as remarkable, including exquisitely furnished chambers, elaborate wood carvings, and breathtaking murals.

Folklore and Legends

Legends and mythology abound around Corvin Castle, as they do around many medieval castles. The story of the Turkish prince Vlad the Impaler, who is said to have been imprisoned in the castle's dungeons, is among the most well-known stories connected to the structure.

Visiting Corvin Castle

Visitors may tour Corvin Castle's medieval halls and chambers today since it is accessible to the public. A museum featuring local history and displays on medieval life and combat is housed in the castle.

4. Râșnov Citadel: A Fortress Above the Clouds

Address: Râșnov Citadel, Râșnov 505400, Romania

The Râșnov Citadel is a medieval stronghold situated atop a rocky hill in the town of Râșnov, providing stunning views of the surrounding landscape. Constructed around the 13th century, the citadel functioned as a tactical fortress for the local governing body.

History of Râșnov Citadel

The Teutonic Knights constructed the Râșnov Citadel as a stronghold to keep off intruders. The fortress was strengthened and extended throughout the ages, becoming a significant defensive installation for the area.

Design and Architecture

The Râșnov Citadel, with its strong walls, defended towers, and well-planned structure, is a striking example of medieval fortification. There are many old structures within the citadel, such as a well, a school, and a church.

Visiting Râșnov Citadel

The Râșnov Citadel's medieval walls and towers are accessible for public exploration today. A narrow trail winds up the hill to the citadel, providing breathtaking vistas of the surrounding landscape as it ascends.

The most famous sites in Transylvania are the medieval fortresses Bran Castle, Peles Castle, Corvin Castle, and Rasnov Citadel, each having a distinct history and charm.

Whether you're drawn to Bran Castle, the legendary home of Dracula, Peles Castle, the royal jewel of Romania, the Gothic splendor of Corvin Castle or the breathtaking views of Rasnov Citadel, visiting these legendary castles and fortresses are sure to be a memorable experience.

Mysterious Legends and Folklore

Transylvania is full of myths and folklore that have captured people's attention for ages due to its rich historical background and varied cultural heritage. The mythology of Transylvania is as mysterious as the province itself, ranging from the legend of Dracula to the long-standing customs of its inhabitants.

Unraveling the Myth Dracula

The most well-known tale connected to Transylvania is that of Dracula, the vampire count made immortal in Bram Stoker's book. Despite being a fictitious figure, Vlad the Impaler, a medieval ruler renowned for his ruthless methods against his adversaries, served as the inspiration for the mythology surrounding Dracula.

The Real Dracula: Vlad the Impaler

Wallachian prince Vlad III, often known as Vlad the Impaler, reigned throughout the fifteenth century. He got his nickname because he liked to execute his opponents brutally, by impaling them on stakes—to make them fearful.

Dracula's Connection to Transylvania

Although Vlad the Impaler never resided in Transylvania, his lore has been associated with the region because of his connections there. Bran Castle, also known as Dracula's Castle, is often associated with Dracula mythology.

Dracula's Legacy

Count Dracula has served as the inspiration for many novels, films, and television series, leaving a lasting impression on popular culture. Even though Dracula is a fictitious figure, his tale has fascinated and intrigued people all over the globe.

Transylvanian Traditions and Folklore

A complex fusion of customs and folklore that represent the region's varied cultural past may also be found in Transylvania. Transylvania's folklore, which ranges from colorful festivals to antiquated superstitions, is a vivid reflection of the traditions and beliefs of its people.

Beliefs and Superstitions

Many superstitions and beliefs, some of which stretch back centuries, are associated with Transylvania. The belief in strigoi, a kind of vampire-like monster that is said to emerge from the tomb at night to punish the living, is one of the most well-known superstitions.

Celebrations and Festivals

Numerous vibrant festivals and celebrations that highlight the area's rich cultural legacy are held across Transylvania. Among the most well-known is the Braşov Junii Festival, which has traditional dance, music, and costumes every spring.

Traditional Crafts and Skills

Traditional crafts and skills from Transylvania that have been handed down through the years are likewise well-known. These crafts, which range from ceramics to woodcarving, are evidence of the rich cultural legacy of the area.

Myths Around the Carpathian Mountains

The Carpathian Mountains, which encircle a large portion of Transylvania, are rich in mythology. There is mystery and interest in the

Carpathians, from mysterious animals to strange woodlands.

The Legend of the Piatra Craiului Mountains

The mythology of the Piatra Craiului Mountains is among the most well-known myths related to the Carpathians. Legend has it that there once lived a formidable dragon in the mountains that tormented the nearby towns until a valiant prince slew it.

The Haunted Forest of Hoia Baciu

The Hoia Baciu Forest is said to be inhabited by ghosts and spirits, according to a well-known mythology connected to the Carpathians. Strange occurrences in the forest, such as inexplicable disappearances and lights that don't seem to belong, are also well-known.

Transylvania's folktales and legends are as varied and mysterious as the country itself. Transylvania's folklore is an intriguing representation of its rich cultural past, ranging from the legend of Dracula to the prehistoric customs of its inhabitants.

Discovering Transylvania's mythology and folklore is bound to be a fascinating experience, whether you're attracted to the region's superstitions or the mystique of the Carpathian Mountains.

Natural Wonders and Outdoor Adventures in Transylvania

Transylvania is renowned for its spectacular natural beauty in addition to its rich history and cultural legacy. Transylvania provides a broad choice of outdoor experiences for nature lovers and outdoor enthusiasts, from the magnificent heights of the Carpathian Mountains to the mysterious depths of its caverns.

Hiking in the Carpathian Mountains

Many of Transylvania's hiking options are found in the Carpathian Mountains, one of Europe's top hiking destinations. Hikers of all ability levels will find nirvana in the

Carpathians with their untamed peaks, thick forests, and attractive valleys.

Popular Hiking Trails

- Winding across the Făgăraș Mountains and providing breathtaking views of the surrounding area, the Transfăgărășan Highway is one of the most well-liked hiking pathways in the Carpathians.
- The Piatra Craiului Ridge is another well-liked path that provides sweeping views of the surrounding hills and valleys.

Nature and Wildlife

There is a wide variety of fauna in the Carpathian Mountains, such as wolves, bears, lynx, and wild boar. Numerous plant species, including alpine flowers and rare orchids, may be found in the highlands.

Tips for Hiking in the Carpathians

- The weather in the mountains may be unpredictable, so it's crucial to pack for any changes in the weather while trekking in the Carpathians.
- It is essential to show consideration for the indigenous fauna and adhere to officially approved paths to preserve the delicate alpine ecology.

Exploring Caves in Transylvania

Several intriguing caves in Transylvania are accessible for public exploration. Transylvania's caves provide a unique window into the region's geological past, with attractions like the breathtaking formations of the Bears' Cave and the frightening subterranean environment of the Scărişoara Ice Cave.

Scărişoara Ice Cave

One of the biggest ice caves in the world is the Scărişoara Ice Cave, which is situated in the Apuseni Mountains. The cave is a fascinating place for tourists to explore since it is home to a giant ice structure that is over 10,000 years old.

The Bears' Cave

The Bears' Cave, which is close to Chiscau, got its name from the ancient bear bones that were found there. The cave is well-liked by spelunkers and nature lovers because it has beautiful stalactites and stalagmites.

Wildlife Watching in the National Parks of Transylvania

Numerous diverse national parks and ecological reserves may be found throughout

Transylvania. The national parks of Transylvania provide a rare chance to see some of the most famous species in Europe in their native environments, from the wild horses of the Danube Delta to the brown bears of the Fagaras Mountains.

The Făgăraş Mountains National Park

The Făgăraş Mountains National Park, which is situated in the southern Carpathian Mountains, is home to wolves, lynxes, and wild boar in addition to brown bears. The park is a well-liked spot for birdwatchers as it is home to several bird species.

The Danube Delta Biosphere Reserve

The Danube Delta Biosphere Reserve, one of Europe's biggest wetland regions, is situated in southern Transylvania. It is home to a wide variety of animals, including otters, pelicans, and wild horses. The reserve is a well-liked spot for birdwatching, with records of over 300 different kinds of birds.

Discovering Transylvania's rich natural history is made possible by the region's outdoor activities and natural attractions. Enjoying activities like hiking in the Carpathian Mountains, discovering Transylvanian caverns, or seeing animals in Transylvania's national parks will leave you spellbound by the region's natural beauty and variety.

Hidden Gems and Off the Beaten Path Transylvania

A place of captivating beauty and rich cultural legacy, Transylvania is home to undiscovered treasures that are just waiting to be found. You'll discover real Transylvanian villages, lesser-known castles and fortifications, and lively rural marketplaces with handcrafted products away from the busy towns and tourist masses.

Realistic Villages in Transylvania

Many charming villages in Transylvania provide an insight into traditional Transylvanian life. These towns provide a unique perspective into the region's cultural past and are a joy to visit with their attractive streets, architecture, and amiable residents.

Saschiz

Saschiz is a stunningly maintained medieval settlement in the center of Transylvania that is home to many ancient structures, such as a 14th-century castle and a fortified church. The village is renowned for producing traditional handicrafts including weaving and ceramics.

Biertan

A UNESCO World Heritage Site, Biertan is a town in Transylvania known for its fortified church. The village is a well-liked travel destination for tourists wishing to experience real Transylvanian living because of its stunning surroundings and traditional Transylvanian architecture.

Lesser-known Fortresses and Castles

Although Peles Castle and Bran Castle are the most well-known castles in Transylvania, there are many more equally remarkable fortifications and castles in the area. History buffs should not miss these undiscovered treasures, which provide a window into Transylvania's medieval past.

1. Deva Fortress

Address: Strada Cetății, Deva 337450, Romania

Deva fortification is a 13th-century medieval fortification perched high atop a hill overlooking the city of Deva. The stronghold has many ancient structures, such as a church and a prison, and provides breathtaking views of the surrounding landscape.

2. Rupea Citadel

Address: Strada Cetății, Rupea 505500, Romania

The 14th-century Rupea fortification is a well-preserved medieval fortification close to the town of Rupea. The stronghold is well-liked by tourists wishing to learn more about Transylvania's medieval past since it is bordered by lovely vineyards and provides sweeping views of the surrounding area.

Artisanal Crafts and Local Markets

There is a thriving artisanal sector in Transylvania, where a wide range of traditional crafts and goods are on display at local markets. These fairs provide a special chance to support regional artists and buy genuine Transylvanian goods.

Sibiu Craftsmen's Market

The lively Sibiu Craftsmen's Market, situated in the city's historic center, is a place where regional artists display their traditional crafts, including weaving, woodcarving, and pottery making. When wanting to buy genuine

Transsylvanian souvenirs, tourists often visit this market.

Brasov Artisanal Market

The Artisanal Market in Brasov, another well-liked marketplace in Transylvania, offers a range of handcrafted goods, such as jewelry, textiles, and pottery. You may get some very amazing goods and souvenirs from Transylvania at the market.

Discovering the undiscovered treasures of Transylvania provides an exceptional chance to delve into the area's genuine customs and legacy. You'll be enthralled by the charm and beauty of this wonderful area whether you're seeing real Transylvanian towns, learning about lesser-known castles and fortifications, or looking through neighborhood markets with handcrafted goods.

Culinary Delights of Transylvania

Transylvania is renowned for its mouthwatering cuisine in addition to its breathtaking scenery and extensive history. The food of the area is a distinctive and savory fusion of traditional Romanian meals with Turkish, German, and Hungarian culinary influences.

Traditional Romanian Cuisines

Romanian traditional food is rich and substantial, with an emphasis on using seasonal, fresh ingredients. Along with a variety of herbs and spices, main components in Romanian cuisine include pig, beef, lamb, potatoes, and cabbage. The following are a few of the most well-liked Romanian dishes:

- **Sarmales:** Sarmales are filled cabbage rolls with a savory mixture of rice, ground pork, and spices; they are often eaten with sour cream.

- **Mămăligă:** A classic cornmeal polenta from Romania that is often eaten as a side dish with stews or other meat dishes.

- **Ciorba:** A sour soup flavored with sour cream and herbs that is cooked with vegetables and either meat or fish.

- **Mititei:** Sausages cooked on a grill using a blend of ground beef, spices, and garlic; often eaten with bread and mustard.

Must-Try Dishes and Local Specialties

Apart from the said traditional foods, Transylvania is renowned for its regional delicacies. In Transylvania, some of the must-try foods and local delicacies are as follows:

- **Varza a la Cluj:** Varza a la Cluj is a classic Transylvanian meal that is often served with sour cream. It is created with cabbage that has been filled with a flavorful combination of minced pork, rice, and spices.

- **Salata de Vinete:** A tasty eggplant salad that's often spread over bread and created with roasted eggplant, onions, garlic, and mayonnaise.

- **Papanași:** Fried dough covered with jam and sour cream, a traditional delicacy in Romania that is often offered as a sweet treat.

Wine Tasting in the Vineyards of Transylvania

Numerous vineyards and wineries in Transylvania create a range of wines, including red, white, and rose varieties. One of the most well-liked activities for tourists interested in experiencing the wine culture of Transylvania is wine tasting. Transylvania has several well-known wine areas, including:

- **Dealul Mare:** Known for its red wines, Dealul Mare is one of Romania's oldest and most prestigious wine areas. It is situated in the southern region of Transylvania.

- **Tarnave:** The Tarnave area, in central Transylvania, is well-known for its Riesling and Pinot Gris white wines.

- **Valea Calugareasca:** This region, which is in northern Transylvania, is well-known for its sparkling wines, especially Feteasca Regala and Alba.

The rich and tasty cuisine of Transylvania offers a unique experience that honors the region's cultural past. You will be pleased by the gastronomic wonders of this lovely area whether you are having a wine tasting in Transylvania's vineyards, sampling local delicacies, or indulging in classic Romanian meals.

8-Day Travel Itinerary in Transylvania

With its breathtaking scenery, intriguing history, and dynamic culture, Transylvania has a lot to offer tourists. A 10-day vacation to Transylvania includes touring historic castles and fortresses, trekking in the Carpathian Mountains, and dining on traditional Romanian cuisine. It promises to be an experience of a lifetime.

Day 1: Arrival in Cluj-Napoca

- When you get to Transylvania's biggest city, Cluj-Napoca, check into your hotel.
- Explore the city's historic core, which has vibrant cafés, museums, and stunning architecture, throughout the day. Don't pass up the opportunity to see

the Ethnographic Museum and the Botanical Garden.

Day 2: Cluj-Napoca to Sibiu

- Leave Cluj-Napoca and go to Sibiu, another charming Transylvanian city.
- Visit the intriguing subterranean site known as the Turda Salt Mine along the route.
- Explore Sibiu's historic district, pay a visit to the Brukenthal National Museum, and meander around its charming lanes.

Day 3: Day Trip From Sibiu

- Spend a day excursion from Sibiu to the neighboring town of Biertan, which has a fortified church that is designated by UNESCO.

- After seeing the settlement and its environments, spend the evening back in Sibiu.

Day 4: Sibiu to Sighișoara

- Go from Sibiu to Sighișoara, a UNESCO World Heritage Site and a stunningly preserved medieval village.
- Stroll the cobblestone streets, see the Clock Tower, and explore the town's historic core.

Day 5: Sighișoara to Brașov

- Travel to Brașov, a charming village tucked away in the Carpathian Mountains, after leaving Sighisoara.
- Make a stop at Viscri's fortified church, another UNESCO-listed landmark, along the route. Take a stroll around the city

walls, discover Brasov's historic core, and pay a visit to the Black Church.

Day 6: Brașov

- Take a day to see Brasov and its environments.
- Take a tour to the neighboring Bran Castle, which is often connected to the Dracula mythology, and discover the surrounding landscape.

Day 7: Brașov to Sinaia

- Proceed to Sinaia, a tourist town renowned for its magnificent Peles Castle, from Brasov.
- Explore the town, go to the castle, and wander around the lovely gardens.

Day 8: Departure From Sinaia

After your 8-day tour in Transylvania, depart from Sinaia.

Take with you memories of this mysterious region's breathtaking scenery, fascinating history, and lively culture as you go.

An 8-day vacation to Transylvania is a great way to take in all of the sights and activities the area has to offer. Transylvania has a lot to offer tourists of all stripes, from charming towns and breathtaking natural settings to medieval castles and fortifications. So gather your belongings and set off on an adventure through this magical area, where fresh and intriguing sides of Romania's rich cultural past are revealed around every turn.

Tour Agencies in Transylvania

Travelers may enjoy a multitude of activities in Transylvania thanks to its captivating culture, breathtaking scenery, and extensive history. A travel agency can assist you in creating the ideal schedule, whether your interests include discovering historic castles, trekking through the Carpathian Mountains, or dining on traditional Romanian food.

1. Transylvania Live

Address: Razboieni Street, 31 A, 401189, Turda, Cluj County, Transylvania, Romania

Transylvania Live focuses on adventure trips, cultural tours, and special events in Transylvania. They let you experience the finest that Transylvania has to offer with a variety of trips, such as Dracula tours, hiking tours, and cultural tours.

2. Active Travel

Address: Strada Diaconu Coresi 2, Brașov 500025, Romania

Adventure travel in Transylvania is the specialty of Active Travel tour agency. They provide a range of trips that let you experience the breathtaking scenery and unspoiled beauty of the area, such as hiking, cycling, and horseback riding experiences.

3. Transylvanian Wonders

Address: Strada Valea Porții 2, Bran 507025, Romania

Transylvanian Wonders focuses on Transylvania's cultural and historical trips. They provide a variety of trips that let you take in the rich history and culture of the area, such as wine tours, castle tours, and village tours.

4. Adventure Transylvania

Address: Satu Mare - Romania

Adventure Transylvania focuses on adventure travel in Transylvania. They provide a range of trips, including rafting, cycling, and hiking tours, so you can take in the breathtaking scenery and outdoor pursuits of the area.

5. Romania Tour Store

Address: Bulevardul Theodor Pallady 18, Bucharest 032263, Romania

Transylvania excursions are among the specialties of Romania Tour Store. They let you experience the finest that Romania has to offer with a range of trips, such as adventure, cultural, and special interest tours.

A firm specializing in tours in Transylvania can assist you in organizing the ideal trip, whether your interests include discovering historic castles, hiking across the Carpathian Mountains, or dining on real Romanian food.

They can help you make the most of your stay in this fascinating area with their experience and local knowledge, making your trip fun and unforgettable. Why then wait? Get in touch with one of these travel companies right now to begin planning your next trip to Transylvania!

Accommodation Options in Transylvania

There are many different lodging alternatives available for visitors visiting Transylvania because of the region's breathtaking scenery, fascinating history, and lively culture. Transylvania has lodging options to fit every taste and budget, whether you're searching for a luxury hotel, a picturesque guesthouse, or an affordable hostel.

Hotels

There are many different kinds of hotels in Transylvania, including boutique hotels, luxury resorts, and affordable lodging alternatives. Hotels in Transylvania are a popular option for tourists searching for a convenient and pleasant location to stay since they provide a variety of amenities, such as restaurants, bars, and spa services. In Transylvania, there are a few hotels that include:

1. Kronwell Brașov Hotel

Address: Bulevardul Gării 7, Brasov 500203, Romania.

Situated in the center of Brasov, this contemporary hotel has stylish accommodations, a rooftop deck, and a spa.

2. Grand Hotel Napoca

Address: Strada Octavian Goga 1, Cluj-Napoca 400698, Romania.

Situated in the heart of Cluj-Napoca, this classy hotel has large rooms, a restaurant, and a fitness facility.

3. Hotel Casa Wagner Brașov

Address: Piața Sfatului 5, Brașov 500031, Romania.

In the heart of Brasov's old district, this little hotel offers comfortable accommodations and a hearty Romanian breakfast.

4. Hilton Sibiu

Address: Strada Pădurea Dumbrava 1, Sibiu 550399, Romania.

This luxury hotel offers breathtaking views of Sibiu's medieval Town. After a long day of traveling, the hotel's exquisite rooms, rooftop bar, and spa are the ideal places to unwind.

Guesthouses

In Transylvania, guesthouses are a common choice for lodging since they provide a more private and individualized experience than hotels. In Transylvania, guesthouses are often family-owned and provide a cozy, friendly environment. Transylvania's top guesthouses include the following:

1. Pensiunea Citadela

Address: Strada Cetății 17, Sighișoara 545400, Romania.

In the center of the historic citadel of Sighisoara, this family-run guesthouse offers cozy accommodations with breathtaking views of the surrounding countryside.

2. Pensiunea Cetate

Address: Strada Stadion 4, Deva 330048, Romania.

This charming guesthouse, which has a garden patio and comfortable rooms, is close to Rasnov Citadel.

3. Pensiunea Eugenia

Address: Strada Profesor Ioan Clinciu 24, Bran 507025, Romania

This little guesthouse, which is close to Bran Castle, has nice accommodations and serves a typical Romanian breakfast.

Hostels

In Transylvania, hostels provide shared amenities and dormitory-style accommodations at an affordable price. For tourists on a tight budget who want to meet other travelers and see the area without breaking the bank, hostels in Transylvania are an excellent option. In Transylvania, some of the top hostels are as follows:

1. Transylvania Hostel
Address: Strada Iuliu Maniu 26, Cluj-Napoca 400095, Romania.
This welcoming hostel with dorm-style rooms and a shared kitchen is situated in the center of Cluj-Napoca.

2. Hostel Boemia
Address: Brasov 500025, Romania.

This little hostel offers dormitory-style accommodations and a friendly environment in Brasov's old center.

There are many different places to stay in Transylvania, including stylish hotels, picturesque guesthouses, and affordable hostels. Transylvania offers lodging options that cater to all budgets and tastes, whether you're searching for a cozy and handy place to stay or something more individualized and private. Why then wait? Begin arranging your travel to Transylvania right now to experience its allure and splendor.

Festivals and Events in Transylvania 2024

Transylvania, a region renowned for its lively customs and rich cultural legacy, hosts a range of festivals and events that highlight the distinct beauty and charm of the area. Transylvania provides a wide variety of events for visitors to enjoy, from music and art festivals to medieval reenactments and customs.

1. Untold Festival (August 8-11, 2024 - Cluj-Napoca)

Held in Cluj-Napoca every year, the Untold Festival is one of the biggest electronic music events in Europe. Against the background of Cluj-Napoca's ancient architecture, an extraordinary roster of international DJs and musicians will perform across numerous stages throughout the event. Untold Festival is a must-visit for both music enthusiasts and festival-goers since it also provides a variety of art installations, workshops, and cultural activities.

2. Sibiu International Theater Festival (June 21-30, 2024 - Sibiu)

One of the most prominent theater events globally is the Sibiu International Theater Festival, which features a wide variety of performances by national and international performers. The festival, which takes place in Sibiu's old core, which is recognized as a UNESCO World Heritage Site, turns the city into a thriving center of theatrical creation. Performances are held in the city's theaters, squares, and streets.

3. Medieval Festival (July 26-28, 2024 - Sighișoara)

Sighisoara's Medieval Festival honors the town's medieval past with reenactments, parades, and festivities centered on the Middle Ages happening all weekend long. With performers enacting historical Sighisoara figures, musicians playing medieval music, and craftsmen showcasing traditional crafts, visitors may fully immerse themselves in the sights and sounds of medieval life.

4. Transilvania International Film Festival (June 14-23, 2024 - Cluj-Napoca)

One of the biggest film festivals in Eastern Europe is the Transilvania International Film Festival (TIFF), which features a wide selection of international films. The festival includes talks with filmmakers, seminars, workshops, and screenings of documentaries, short films, and feature films. Not only does TIFF include a wide range of cultural activities, but it's also a must-see for fans of both culture and movies.

5. Brasov International Marathon (June 01-02, 2024 - Brasov)

A two-day running competition, the Brasov International Marathon draws competitors from all over the globe. There are other events held throughout the marathon, such as a family run, a half marathon, and a 10K race. The marathon offers a unique approach to taking in the beauty of the area as it winds through Brasov's charming towns and the surrounding countryside.

The festivals and events of Transylvania provide a special chance to discover the rich cultural legacy of the area. 2024 promises to be a delightful and inspiring year for everyone visiting Transylvania, whether it is a theatergoer, music lover, or just someone seeking a taste of the local warmth. So be sure to put Transylvania in your calendars, pack your luggage, and get ready to explore its many fascinating festivals and events in 2024.

Practical Information for Travelers in Transylvania

Travelers find Transylvania to be an intriguing destination because of its captivating scenery and rich cultural legacy. Being ready with useful knowledge on safety, emergency contacts, and currencies can guarantee a simple and pleasurable journey.

Currency and Money Matters

The Romanian Leu (RON) is the country's official currency. To meet urgent needs, it is advised to convert some cash before traveling to Transylvania. Major cities and villages have plenty of ATMs where you may use your debit or credit card to withdraw cash. While most hotels, restaurants, and stores take credit cards, it's a good idea to have cash on hand for minor purchases or unexpected expenses.

General and Safety Tips

Although Transylvania is a relatively safe place to visit, you should always take safety steps to be sure. The following general advice should be remembered:

- Be mindful of your surroundings and safeguard your belongings, particularly in busy settings.
- Refrain from flaunting expensive or substantial sums of cash in public.
- Use caution while using public transit, and avoid going somewhere by yourself late at night.
- When visiting holy locations, observe local customs and traditions and dress modestly.

Emergency Contacts

It's critical to know who to call for help in an emergency. The following emergency numbers are helpful in Romania:

Emergency Services (Fire, Ambulance, Police): 112

Medical Facilities in Transylvania

In the event of an emergency or health problem, it's important to know about the medical facilities in the enchanted area of Transylvania. Like any other holiday location, Transylvania offers a variety of medical services, like hospitals, and pharmacies, to guarantee your well-being and safety while you're away from home.

Hospitals

Transylvania's hospitals are prepared to treat a variety of illnesses and medical emergencies. Among the primary medical facilities in Transylvania are:

1. County Emergency Hospital Cluj-Napoca
Address: Strada Clinicilor 3-5, Cluj-Napoca 400006, Romania.
Offering a variety of medical services and specializations, this hospital is among the biggest and best-equipped in Cluj-Napoca.

2. General Hospital Sibiu
Address: Bulevardul Corneliu Coposu 2-4, Sibiu 550245, Romania
This hospital is a significant healthcare center in Sibiu that offers both locals and visitors emergency and specialty medical services.

3. Municipal Emergency Hospital Brasov

Address: Calea București 25, Brașov 500326, Romania

With a comprehensive variety of medical services and treatments available, this hospital is a top healthcare center in Brasov.

Pharmacies

Transylvania has a large number of well-stocked pharmacies that provide an extensive selection of pharmaceuticals and medical supplies. Among the main drugstore chains in Transylvania are:

1. Catena Pharmacy

Address: Piața Victoriei 4, Timișoara 300006, Romania

One of the biggest drugstore chains in Romania, Catena has outlets in all of Transylvania's main cities and villages.

2. Sensiblu Pharmacy

Address: Piața Victoriei 7, Timișoara 300030, Romania

Another significant drugstore chain in Romania that sells a variety of prescription drugs and medical supplies is called Sensiblu.

Travelers may enjoy tons of experiences in the fascinating country of Transylvania. You can guarantee seamless and delightful travel in this fascinating area by being ready with useful information like emergency contacts and medical facilities, safety precautions, and currencies. Transylvania promises to be an amazing and fulfilling vacation destination, whether you want to hike in the Carpathian Mountains, explore ancient castles, or enjoy traditional Romanian food.

Useful Phrases in Romanian

Understanding a few simple words in Romanian can help you converse with locals and improve your trip to Transylvania. Even if English is widely spoken in Transylvania, attempting to speak the local tongue may be quite valued.

Greetings and Basic Phrases

Hello: Buna ziua (BOO-nuh ZEE-wah)

Goodbye: La revedere (LAH reh-veh-DEH-reh)

Yes: Da (DAH)

No: Nu (NOO)

Please: Va rog (vuh ROHG)

Thank you: Multumesc (mool-tzoo-MESK)

You're welcome: Cu placere (koo

pluh-CHER-eh)

Excuse me: Scuzati-ma (SKOO-zuh-tee MAH)

I'm sorry: Imi pare rau (EE-mee PAH-reh row)

Getting Around

Where is...?: Unde este...? (OON-deh YES-teh)

How much is...?: Cat costa...? (KAHT KOSS-tah)

Can you help me?: Puteti sa ma ajutati?

(poo-TEH-tee sah mah ah-zhoo-TAHT-see)

I don't understand: Nu inteleg (NOO

een-TEH-leg)

Eating and Drinking

I would like...: As vrea... (ahss VREH-ah)

A table for two, please: O masa pentru doi, va

rog (oh MAH-sah pehn-TRU DOY, vuh ROHG)

The bill, please: Nota de plata, va rog (NOH-tah

deh PLAH-tah, vuh ROHG)

Cheers!: Noroc! (noh-ROHK)

Emergencies

Help!: Ajutor! (ah-ZHOO-tor)

I need a doctor: Am nevoie de un doctor (ahm neh-VOY deh oon DOHK-tohr)

Where is the nearest hospital?: Unde este cel mai apropiat spital? (OON-deh YES-teh chel my ah-PROH-pyat SPEE-tahl)

General Advice

- In Romanian, words are spoken phonetically, meaning they are pronounced exactly as they are written.
- Shaking hands is customary while saying hello to someone. Family members and close friends may give each other cheek kisses.

- Addressing someone with their title (Domnul for Mr. and Doamna for Mrs./Ms.) and last name is considered courteous.

Learn these practical Romanian words so you can improve your Transylvanian vacation experience and converse with locals more efficiently. Even though English is often spoken in tourist locations, attempting to communicate in the local tongue will greatly enhance your trip through this fascinating place by helping you make lasting memories and significant relationships.

Frequently Asked Questions About Transylvania

If you're a tourist who's thinking about visiting Transylvania, you probably have a lot of questions about this intriguing area. Gaining a knowledge of Transylvania may improve your experience and help you make the most of your trip, from its history and culture to useful travel advice.

1. Where is Transylvania located?

A historical area in central Romania, Transylvania is bounded to the east and south by the Carpathian Mountains. It is renowned for its rich cultural history, medieval towns, and breathtaking natural scenery.

2. When is the ideal time of year to visit Transylvania?

A visit to Transylvania is best planned at your discretion. Summertime (June to August) is a popular time for festivals and outdoor activities, although it may become congested. Both the fall (September to October) and spring (April to May) seasons provide nice weather and fewer people. For those who like snow activities, winter (November to March) is great.

3. How do I get to Transylvania?

You may get to Transylvania via bus, rail, and airplane. With links to important European cities, Cluj-Napoca, Sibiu, and Timisoara are home to the region's three main airports. Transylvania is connected to neighboring regions of Romania and Europe via bus and train services.

4. Is English a common language in Transylvania?

Younger generations in Transylvania speak English in tourism regions. Still, knowing a few simple words in Romanian might come in handy and be well-received by the people there.

5. What are the must-see attractions in Transylvania?

There are a lot of must-see sights in Transylvania, such as Peles Castle, Sibiu's ancient town, Biertan, and Viscri fortified churches, and Bran Castle, which is connected to the Dracula legend.

6. Is traveling to Transylvania safe?

A: Travelers may feel comfortable visiting Transylvania in general. Still, it's wise to use common sense, such as locking up your belongings and paying attention to your surroundings.

7. What currency is in use in Transylvania?

The Romanian Leu (RON) is the currency in use in Transylvania. It's best to exchange some money ahead of time since there are fewer ATMs in remote locations.

8. What is essential to bring while traveling to Transylvania?

Arrange your belongings based on the season and the things you want to accomplish. Essentials include sunscreen, weather-appropriate clothes, comfortable walking shoes, and a camera. Bring the right equipment if you want to trek.

9. Are there any Transylvanian cultural traditions that I should be aware of?

It's crucial to honor regional traditions and customs in Transylvania. Wear modest clothing when you visit churches or monasteries. A handshake is often exchanged during greetings, and it's courteous to address someone by their title (domnul for Mr. and doamna for Mrs./Ms.) and then their last name.

10. What are some traditional dishes to try when visiting Transylvania?

The food of Transylvania is renowned for being tasty and hearty. Try the typical fare of cozonac (sweet bread), mamaliga (polenta), and sarmale (cabbage rolls packed with meat and rice).

Transylvania is a captivating tourist destination since it is an area rich in culture, history, and scenic beauty. You can make sure that your trip to this fascinating area of Romania is memorable and pleasurable by being aware of the topography, points of interest, and cultural practices of the area.

Conclusion

Reflecting on Your Transylvanian Adventure

As your trip to Transylvania draws to an end, pause to consider the amazing experiences and memories you have made. With its breathtaking scenery, fascinating history, and dynamic culture, Transylvania has probably had a lasting effect on you.

You have many treasured memories from your trip to Transylvania, including hiking in the Carpathian Mountains, discovering medieval castles and fortresses, and enjoying traditional Romanian food.

Advice for Future Travelers

1. Plan Ahead: Make an itinerary based on your research on the sights and activities you're interested in. This will guarantee that you don't miss any must-see places and help you make the most of your stay in Transylvania.

2. Be Respectful: When visiting places of worship, dress modestly and show consideration for the customs and traditions of the area. Respecting the local way of life may also be shown by learning a few simple Romanian words.

3. Remain Safe: Although Transylvania is a relatively safe place to visit, you should still take safety measures. Be mindful of your surroundings and safeguard your belongings, particularly in busy settings.

4. Try Local Cuisine: Don't pass up the chance to experience the tasty and hearty traditional Romanian food. Try some of the delicacies, such as mici (grilled buns with minced pork) and sarmale (cabbage rolls).

5. Discover Off the Beaten Path: While Transylvania's main towns and tourist destinations are undoubtedly worthwhile visits, don't be scared to stray off the main road and discover some of the area's lesser-known treasures. You might find something that surprises you.

6. Embrace the Great Outdoors: Transylvania's breathtaking natural settings are a must-see throughout every trip. Make sure to spend some time outside taking in the splendor of this enchanted country, whether you're hiking in the Carpathian Mountains, discovering the region's caves, or seeing animals in its national parks.

7. Make Friends with Locals: Getting to know the people of Transylvania is a great approach to discovering the region's authentic essence. Having a discussion with a shopkeeper or going on a tour with a local guide are two excellent ways to get insight into the history and culture of the area.

Transylvania has been an adventure for you, full of breathtaking scenery, fascinating cultural interactions, and brand-new experiences. Take the memories you've made with you and hold onto them for years to come as you think back on your stay in this magical area.

I hope your travels bring you wonderful experiences and fresh discoveries, whether you're heading back to Transylvania or exploring other places. La revedere, or farewell, till we meet again, and have safe travels!

Happy Traveling

Printed in Great Britain
by Amazon